STEPRO BOOKS

ON THE TRIPOD

ON THE TRIPOD

"If the photographer is interested in the people in front of his lens, and if he is compassionate, it's already a lot. The instrument is not the camera but the photographer."
— **Eve Arnold**

Tak Jm

te rad

DEFs

CPSIA information can be obtained
at www.ICGtesting.com
Printed in the USA
BVHW050444210819
556215BV00045B/1388/P

9 780464 196396